Invocation

Invocation

Wally Swist

LAMAR UNIVERSITY
LITERARY PRESS

ISBN: 978-1-942956-12-9
Library of Congress Control Number: 2015950311

Manufactured in the United States

Lamar University Literary Press
Beaumont, Texas

Acknowledgments

I am grateful to the editors of the following publications for publishing some of the poems in this collection:

Alimentum: The Literature of Food
All Roads Will Lead You Home
Appalachia
Blessing and Homage
Blood and Honey Review
Bliss
Blue Lyra Review
Blueline
Buddhist Poetry Review
The Cape Rock
Common Ground Review
Commonweal
Connecticut River Review
Crab Orchard Review
Connotation Press: An Online Archive
Dappled Things: A Quarterly of Ideas, Art, & Faith
EarthSpeak
Empirical Magazine
The Galway Review (Ireland)
The Guidebook
Halcyon (Canada)
The Loft Anthology: New England Poetry and Art
Literatura ir Menas (Lithuania)
Many Hands: A Magazine for Holistic Health
Miramar
Noctua Review
North American Review
Perfume River Poetry Journal
Poetry Salzburg (Austria)
Prosopisia (India)
Pushing the Envelope: Epistolary Poems
Rattle
Still Point Arts Quarterly
String Poets

Theodate
The Tule Review
The Wayfarer: A Journal of Contemplative Literature
The Whirlwind Review
Wild River Review
Written River

"Wild Falling" was selected to be printed on a granite column in Edmands Park in Newton, Massachusetts, as part of the city's Poetry in the Park Project.

I am grateful to the following literary agencies for granting financial assistance while some of these poems were written:

The Authors League Fund
PEN America
Poets in Need, which awarded me a Philip Whalen Memorial Grant

For the Readers of These Poems

Poetry from Lamar University Literary Press

Alan Berecka, *With Our Baggage*
David Bowles, *Flower, Song, Dance: Aztec and Mayan Poetry*
Jerry Bradley, *Crownfeathers and Effigies*
Paul Christensen, *The Jack of Diamonds is a Hard Card to Play*
Chip Dameron, *Waiting for an Etcher*
William Virgil Davis, *The Bones Poems*
Jeffrey DeLotto, *Voices Writ in Sand*
Mimi Ferebee, *Wildfires and Atmospheric Memories*
Larry Griffin, *Cedar Plums*
Ken Hada, *Margaritas and Redfish*
Michelle Hartman, *Disenchanted and Disgruntled*
Michelle Hartman, *Irony and Irreverence*
Katherine Hoerth, *Goddess Wears Cowboy Boots*
Lynn Hoggard, *Motherland*
Gretchen Johnson, *A Trip Through Downer, Minnesota*
Ulf Kirchdorfer, *Chewing Green Leaves*
Janet McCann, *The Crone at the Casino*
Erin Murphy, *Ancilla*
Laurence Musgrove, *Local Bird*
Dave Oliphant, *The Pilgrimage, Selected Poems: 1962-2012*
Kornelijus Platelis, *Solitary Architectures*
Carol Coffee Reposa, *Underground Musicians*
Jan Seale, *The Parkinson Poems*
Carol Smallwood, *Water, Earth, Air, Fire, and Picket Fences*
Glen Sorestad *Hazards of Eden*
W.K. Stratton, *Ranchero Ford/ Dying in Red Dirt Country*
Wally Swist, *Invocation*
Jonas Zdanys (ed.), *Pushing the Envelope, Epistolary Poems*

For information on Lamar University Press books go to
www.Lamar.edu/LiteraryPress

CONTENTS

All mystics speak the same language,
for they come from the same country.
—Louis-Claude de Saint-Martin

Ode to February

Sweet onions and sardines browned in a skillet in olive oil,
served with the blessing of two day-old baguette and a glass

from a bottle of an affordable Cotes-Du-Rhone, is the closest
I may ever come to *Tushita Heaven*, as I listen to the pouring

winter rain, and am aware I need little else that compares
with *just this* and these blue lights that flash in their nests

of snow shadow from the slow moving traffic I watch
from the front windows of the farmhouse that face the road.

Montepulciano and Caravaggio

I have thought about you tonight in my savoring a glass, or two,
of a delicious Montepulciano D'Abruzzo (Vendemmia 2008),

along with a double-cream Brie. However, it would have been
better paired with a Gorgonzola, but I am not complaining.

This particular Montepulciano offers such a rich palette
of various layers of dark cherry, and spice laced with purple plum,

that open out across the tongue, and in tasting it I imagine
I could be viewing a still life by Caravaggio, and concomitantly

sharing in the portion of the abundance spread
across the table in the light from beyond the edges of the painting.

The last sentence is an example of what is known as paratactic
syntax, that is sometimes attributed to the adaptation

of Oriental poetry in English, in which two dissimilar
images, or fragments, are juxtaposed without any direct connection

of one statement with the other, such as: It is snowing tonight,
and I will step into the storm to sit beneath the white candelabra

of the branches of the Kousa dogwood. Perhaps a better example is:
Tomorrow I will walk across the snowy fields, and when I stop

by the river in the sunlight, I will think of Caravaggio
and taste the Montepulciano I drank last night

but not the Gorgonzola I did not complain being without,
since I deferred to my humility, and left it in the painting.

Bloodroot Open before Trillium

Whatever it was I lost, whatever I wept for
Was a wild, gentle thing, the small dark eyes
Loving me in secret.
                        —James Wright

Last of the snow melt
        drips from the sodden, mossy cliffs—
                yellow bands of sunlight stippling

the fresh spring greens.
        Water sound rises from the gorge—
                the brook tumbling down the slope

before it races over boulders
        at the chute of the falls. The wet air
                rinsing my face with its sound.

Beside the mountain trail,
        muddy with runoff, the race
                of the brook quickens into a pool,

and I am reminded
        of my Grail Castle experience
                when I was thirteen, so like Parsifal,

woods-walking for the first time
        alone, how I sensed *those hidden eyes loving*
                me in secret, James Wright speaks of.

As I hike through the shadows
        of new leaves, the path to the summit
                is littered on both sides with birch,

beech, and hemlock, uprooted after
        the ice storm last December, chain-sawed
                into slash—resin still burning the air.

Blessing

A pair of mourning cloaks drift among the white flowers
of wood anemones and the runners of blossoming

wild strawberry. Fiddleheads unfurl on the slopes,
and trillium, nearly gone past, now resembles its nickname,

Stinking Benjamin, its dried, wrinkled three-pointed
boutonnieres having been pollinated by flies. On the dusty

April trail, far too dry for this time of the year,
a horse's hooves have fractured stones along the path

that litter the rise to the summit, leaving some of them
broken in the shape of a heart. Clusters of Quaker Ladies,

in shoals of blue petals, amid their golden yellow centers,
ripple beside the trailside in a rush of wind. Hillside after

hillside of new foliage, not quite green, begins to leaf out
across the breadth of forest, sloping over the ridges, among

the pines, from the view at the fire tower from Greylock
to Monadnock. Creaking in the wind like the unoiled iron hinges

of a barn door, and returning back into the nothingness
from which it came, a raptor's call issues across an amethyst sky.

Backlit in a Wash of Light
for Art Goodtimes

I think of you writing me last night,
       of your grief. The invisible lead filling
             the interstices between your words:

I'm in San Francisco.
       My brother is dying. It's been
             nearly thirty years since we hiked up

Slaughterhouse Gulch, when you were
       living at the foot in the pine lodge,
             where legend has it Butch Cassidy

practiced jumping onto his horse
       before he robbed the San Miguel
             Valley Bank in Telluride, and rode

out of that box canyon in 1889.
       A mourning cloak leads me, then
             shadows me, on the path, not unlike

you playing *Coyote* back then. We lassoed
       ropes onto the rocky outcrops above
             dry waterfalls on our way to the top

of a mesa that was studded
       orange with poppies; I watched you
             stalk a herd of elk, before we hiked

back down to recross the shallow race
       of that part of the Colorado River.
             Here, on Mount Toby in western

Massachusetts, just beyond
       pine shade and leaf-mold, the petals
             of trailing arbutus begin to flower—

some buds open, others closed;
      all so new among their quickly
           browning leaves. I'm still inhaling

the sweetness of their fragrance
      even after having almost descended
           the trail—then just happen to look

back up the mountain
      slope to see spray from
           the brook backlit in a wash of light.

Tone Poem for Summer Solstice
after Robert Francis

Say oxeye daisy tansy yarrow orange hawkweed
purple clover Say skipper mourning cloak silver-

bordered fritillary monarch clouded sulfur Say
blue-eyed grass blue toadflax ragged robin *rosa*

rugosa shinleaf *pyrola* jewelweed white campion
Say bluebird swallow purple martin Say dragonfly

honey bee bald-faced hornet Say downy brome
curly dock barnyard grass hop clover Say warbler

Summer Palette

*after the paintings of Shirley Fredrickson Conant
and her Burnett Watercolor Show, March 2010*

The resplendent summer immemorial of Down East flora
and clean Edward Hopper-plumb lines of roof and sill,

with the opacity of windows filled with light,
with the clarity of windows reflecting a particular patch

and specific hue of sky, draw us into the periphery
of the landscapes that the artist has chosen for us to walk into.

My favorite, "Blueberry Basket," painted
in Sedgwick, Maine, brims its near-overflow with Taoist

sensibilities, succulent with the delectable fruit
of the highbush shrubs that fringe the meander

of the middle path in an *homage* to the pastels of summer.
The daisies, cinquefoil, and beach plum that flowers

and ripens in each of these canvasses, is an illuminated page
in the wordless Book of Odes in celebration of the rock-ribbed

Maine coast that opens to us with the fragrance of the sea
breeze, with the dunes awash in *rosa rugosa,*

where the Bonsai of rock reflects rock in the ocean
of a single puddle, where the needles of a crooked pine mirror

a forest in the pools of low tide, quaking with
petals of lupine that speckle the ripples and flash in the dusk.

Cinnamon and Honey

after Wolfgang Amadeus Mozart's Clarinet
Concerto in A, Rondo (Allegro), Kochel 622

We have lived most of our lives
Preparing for what it is

We think we have lost—
Before beginning to just come into

Our knowing how the fulfillment
Of consciousness unfolds

Into its own sumptuousness,
Whose pleasure supreme

Offers a similar taste as that of cinnamon,
And how much and how often

We can possibly spread its luscious
Silkiness through emanations

Through and around us,
Flowing like honey from a broken comb,

Like the light irradiating its flow,
And the color of the light imbued

With the honey, and the sweetness
Beyond just a honeyed sweetness,

When the light emanates not only
Around us any sunny morning,

As the walls of the red brick brownstones
Sparkle in a steady stream,

But also swells through us in a confluence
As a river that flows into the sea.

A Field of Sunflowers

La tristesse durera toujours.
                    —Vincent van Gogh

Give up what you want to gain,
          the guide says, as I pass a field
                    of sunflowers, the inflorescence of all of the flower

heads facing east to greet
          the sun; and the one stalk in the rear
                    of the field a corolla-head higher than the rest, making

an offering of itself, as did
          the Buddha, by holding up a single flower,
                    as I find within myself a smile that spreads outward,

similar to Mahakasyapa's smile that
          traced the recognition of true *Self* across his lips.
                    Whether seeming a slight of hand, that magician's trick

of heliotropism, with each sympetalous
          face, a throng of spiritual devotees turns
                    to the sun in unison, alert to the silent *Mullah* calling

the rising of the light. Their flower heads
          are the faces of those just after morning prayers
                    before they rise from their knees beneath the mosque

of blue sky to choose not to enter into
          another day of *Jihad,* and they resemble
                    the faces of those who begin their day in the same fields,

who blend into the marketplace,
          in the midst of the sweetness of their lives,
                    that make a choice to ignite the truck bomb, to detonate

the IED, and as *saboteurs,* whether
          to pull the cord on their suicide belt while standing
                    beside the flower seller's stall. One raft after another

of sunflowers, head to stem, floating
       on their roots, was used to mop up the nuclear spill
            at Chernobyl. Although Vincent, poor man, chose to

perish as he strode through a field
       of *Helianthus*, as he clutched at the canvasses
            he had painted of them, and in placing those paintings

down among a row, aimed a pistol at his chest,
       with what we might imagine as trembling
            hands, then pulled the trigger, wounding himself
                mortally.

Two days later, he died at the Inn at Ravoux,
       not only among the beauty emanating from each
            of their bright faces, but also amid their brilliant
                splendor.

Dream of a Holy City

In the dream, I visited
      a holy city. White-walled, several
            domed buildings were reserved for

the use of practice,
      service, and prayer. They
            were constructed of white alabaster—

all of the architecture
      was smooth, all of it shone.
            What was communicated, wordlessly,

was that it was not my time to be
      there. However, it was made salient,
            that this was home, and this is where

I am to return to. *It is not*
      your time yet, quietly and clearly
            instructed a voice, as I was bathed

in such well-being: a sense
      so palpable, yet so much
            beyond description. Upon waking,

I lay in bed, aware—
      Or was I still dreaming?—
            that your life and mine have been

guided to be together,
      that the geometric lines of
            our meeting were planned sometime

before. I was to know
      this, to understand that we
            are meant to learn from one another,

and in doing so,
        to advance previous capacities
                for becoming, to go beyond what we

had already experienced,
        separately and in unison.
                Only if we allow ourselves, we may

still awaken to
        pre-dawn birdsong, whose
                intermittent flourishes deepen the silence.

Aubade

In revising what I wrote to you, I believe that
tempted is the wrong verb.

Becoming more open
offers the genesis of a more accurate phrase.

Speaking closely with you may be more like
finding bits of the comb in every spoonful of honey.

Your possibly coming to see me
would be a vehicle to a not so perplexing question.

Arising together
could be one of the very best answers.

The Lawrence Durrell *Alexandria Quartet* Mediterranean Cold Plate Dinner Special

The Justine: A pound of chilled broiled salmon,
Marinated in butter and lemon juice.
The Balthazar: Six ears of sweet corn,
Shaved off the cob; one small red onion,

Minced in large pieces, peasant-style;
One can of small white pinto beans; sufficient
Amounts of olive oil and balsamic vinegar; one
Teaspoon of chili powder; mix ingredients; chill.

The Mount Olive: Half a pound of green beans,
Seared *al dente* (medium heat; two to three
Minutes) in olive oil; golden raisins;
Dried sliced apricots, a handful of walnuts;

Abundant chunks of crumbled feta, toss
With a splash or two more of olive oil; chill.
The Clea: One large zucchini, halved, then
Quartered at an angle; seared *al dente* (medium

Heat; three to five minutes, on the flat side);
Allow to cool. (Recommendation:
Drizzle some of the oil from the skillet
Onto the salmon when plating the meal.)

Arrange all of the above, lyrically,
Onto plates, so that each may begin to speak
The truth, in their turn. Suggested beverage:
Iced coffee, with crushed ice and cream,

Or half and half. Alternate beverage
Suggestions for those gentle reprobates
With an interest in a taste of debauchery:
Chilled Spanish Cava *or* Vin de Cassis

(Any chilled inexpensive, dry French white
Wine mixed with no more than a drop or two
Of Creme de Cassis). Serves: Four. Restores
The body and the mind and reinvigorates

The spirit, like the mild but steady wind
Off the ocean at dusk—pungent with that
Piquant kiss of salt in the air that seasons
Each of us to the depth of our very soul.

Rock and Meadow

I enjoyed hearing the anecdote
of her child-self, at eight, when she perched

on the rock that she claimed as a throne
in the meadow near her home,

ruling over her peers in the neighborhood with
her scepter, or rather a part of a deadfall stick.

Now, how wonderful is that? I will never forget it.
How true it is that whole mystical tableau

has transcended itself, in many ways in her life,
and has morphed into the corner office

she now inhabits and works out of, not to mention
so many other forms of her meadow rock

and her eight-year-old child-self.
I can only wish I could stop imagining we were

realized in such a way in our lives: for me to be
that rock for her and for her to be that meadow,

in which she rests upon her throne and watches
the wind's scepter wave over the summer grasses.

Nymphs and Satyr

after a painting by William-Adolphe Bouguereau, 1873

Bouguereau painted the satyr, brought
down by the sisterhood of nymphs, and represented

a mythological truth that otherwise might be
overlooked, especially since he painted the figures

life-size. We can't miss that the satyr in the painting
is in flight, resisting the nymphs

who are in pursuit. Would we to learn to not pass
judgment before considering

the archetypal elements in our own psyche, or even
nature herself? As in the flight-dance

of the scout bee before the hive, she communicates
to her sisters, who await her arrival, exactly where

the nectar-rich blossoms are, and not only
where they have opened within their own sweetness,

but also in what clearing or meadow.
Just as by the lip of what pond, or by which twisting

cataract or waterfall, insouciant nymphs
just may be pursuing the real satyr of our imagination.

Pole Star

Although I have discovered
that poems can offer intimations

of what is sacred, what guides me
is the imminent spirituality

of poetry itself. The path
is where *the Sacred Heart of Jesus,*

the Christ Self, opens, as in
my dream of the white dolphin

that broke the surface of the ocean
and rose out of my own chest.

It is there we are bathed
in the light we have been seeking,

when we just breathe and cease
seeking it—one breath at a time.

Ode to the Mockingbird

Our neighborhood mockingbird and I have
become friends. Whenever I am on the phone,

and standing before the screen door,
the mockingbird hops across

the parqueted brick walk to stare—
it must know my voice by now. If I have

jazz on in the evening, I'll eventually hear
the mockingbird singing to the music.

I'll have to turn my head, or rise from my chair,
and I'll see it soloing, perched on one

of the porch rails, or where the mockingbird
appears to prefer to stand on those bricks

of the walk. I've come to discern that
the mockingbird is also like me, or I like it—

with feathers a bit worn.
My friend has, as have I, survived a few storms.

We exchange a certain tenderness,
as we look at the other, inquisitively.

Never have I enjoyed such camaraderie
with any other bird, especially a mockingbird.

I can even say that we nearly keep
our ears tuned for each other's songs.

Black-eyed Susan

for Susan Gage Tyler

Butter-yellow inflorescence, ballerina's skirt
ruffled in the wind, common sweetheart

of wildflowers, who eschews the solitary
for a throng of other Susans; the brown,

dark-purplish center one of summer's
most obvious, most subtle of baubles.

Double Gold, Indian Summer, Marmalade,
your various shades reveal your inimitable

humor. Leaning wildly windward,
rising in a stand, resting together in the sun,

the summer's lushness no longer lush without
your strong-stemmed, unconstrained bounty—

solstice celebrant, resplendent
Susan among so many Susans.

Blue Chicory

for Paris Finley

Its petals may be described as vivid blue,
but if anything they are the color of the silence

of an early morning summer sky. Unlobed
and pointed leaves spread along its rough,

grooved stem by any roadside. Its nicknames
include *succory* and *coffeeweed*, but my favorite

is *ragged sailor*. In Puglian cuisine, the leaves
of wild chicory are mixed with fava bean puree,

known as *Fave e Cicorie Selvatiche*. Wild chicory
leaves are bitter, but their bitterness can be

reduced if the leaves are boiled. It is also
suggested that they are then sautéed with garlic,

and combined with pasta. The root was
ground and adopted as a coffee substitute

by Confederate soldiers during the Civil War.
Puntarelle, a common meal in Rome, is made

with chicory sprouts. Due to their protein
and fat content, chicory roots have been used

as a desired alternative for horses. According
to European folklore, chicory is also believed

to unlock doors. Although it may be best known
when it is cultivated as radicchio, sugarloaf,

or Belgian endive. After all, Horace wrote:
As for me, olives, endives, and mallows provide.

Let me set my table by chicory's providence,
and lay my dishes out to await its many gifts,

as the shadows of birds pass over my setting
of silverware and plates to disappear

across the sky that, if anything, only
resembles the vivid blue of chicory petals.

Experiencing the Light

Then there were the mornings, when I would set
the table for breakfast and your cat would talk to me

in her feline language of meows, of happy yowls, before
you came down the stairs, and we would smile. It was

at that time you nicknamed me Mr. Man, the one who
spoke with your cat, the one with whom you could

confide in when you might see a window-paned wall
as stained glass, or the time we saw the heron's aura

in the sky above us while picnicking in a hayed summer
meadow. What I will remember best is the light

that emanates and haloes both our faces when we are
together and we let it. What I will always miss

is unbuttoning your blue cardigan, the softness of it,
that opened to the hardness of nipples, and how

I understood what it was to love the body of a woman
after having been with other women over many years,

for the first time. Each time was a nuptial, and every time,
those moments lapsed into their own perpetuity,

like the beatific smoothness of the marble
of a Michelangelo, and the light sculpted in Mary's face

in *La Pieta*, in the creation of something other than
the sculpture itself, there was the light we entered

that our bodies could not exhaust—even the fragrance
of your sweat was sweet to me. What our bodies did

to each other, when you still used to grant them that
blissful abandon, was a revelation beyond prayer.

What I did to break the crystal that held the clarity
of what we held and what held us was my own fear

of breakage, my inadequacy of living in the eternity
of the moment. What humility I have learned, and at

what cost, after having been taught that lesson, I now
know how I could not have lost you, but lost you I have.

When on those occasions we see each other, only by
my own inventive making, it is the ring of our laughter

together that fills any room. It is in experiencing
the light beginning to fill each other's face that makes me

think how easy it would have been to have made
this work each day of our lives, but we would have

needed to have grounded our experience in the divinity
of the everyday, and I believe it is in our seeking

divinity everyday that we have not only lost the art
of being together but also the practice and the path. It is

by your saying that simple *yes* to me when I suggest to you
that what we have had has lasted without lasting.

Natal Chart and Transits
for Donna Overall

I love the phrase you ended your email
      with: *One Life, One Heart, One Love.*
           For years, I would wish *the best of serendipities*

to recipients of my letters. Now, that
      blessing varies, dependent on what
           I discern is appropriate. On New Year's eve,

I want to thank you again, for all
      of the work that you achieved in my behalf
           and for the purposes of my astrological past,

present, and future. What
      the natal chart revealed resonated,
           as might the captain of a debating team's *gerunds*

ringing like the Buddha's gongs—
      or how John McPhee portrays
           the Princeton archeologist that he palled around

with in his book *Basin and Range.*
      What occurred was a deep realization
           of why I am in this life, to begin with. It may be

best explained as coming back
      to the wall one remembers as where
           you started this particular journey, then locating

the door you walked through
      to begin it, that didn't exist until you began
           this specific existence. However, with the transits

for the year, I admit that I read
      the first twelve, as you know, of what are
           fifty-eight pages for the entirety of the coming year.

After so doing, I believe how
        to actually read the transits carefully is
                along with the year itself, and to not become too far

ahead of myself by attempting
        to process the whole set of keys all at once.
                So, I will use the transit reading as a guide, instead

of a leaping off place. Remember
        that the folksinger, Utah Phillips, liked to say,
                Some days you just have to wake up and jump off a cliff.

That might be what's necessary,
        on occasion; however that may not be the surest way
                for me, or anyone, to interpret our astrological truths.

Wild Falling

Eyes frozen in headlights for
only a moment, the herd

of deer traverses the road
in this first winter blizzard

with such prudence they quiet
the wild falling. One after

another, they spring to clear
the ice-sheathed barbed wire hurdle,

that quivers from time to time
when one of their hooves grazes

against it. They bound into
the meadow, filling with white

fire, an icy afterglow
burnishing their tracks, that cross

and re-cross themselves, while wisps
of cloud wash over the moon.

Mink

Standing beside the brook pool that winter
Morning, where I had scattered the ashes

Of my yellow Labrador, bright February sun
Igniting the snowbanks into glare, the sound

Of its nails over the ice crust just beginning
To escalate into a roar, as it adjusted the long

Lithe yard of its stunning black furred body
In its attempt to steer down the slope of one

Bank, then another; sunlight flickering off
The radiant oil of its coat, as it veered,

Appearing to drift uncontrollably, on a line
Straight toward me, so quickly, I didn't even

Think of sidestepping over to the left
Or dodging right, but remember edging

Backward towards the flange of the brook's
Icy ledges. When it was only a few feet away

From me, it angled to its right, and in one
Fluid wildly acrobatic motion, leapt, after

Taking several running steps, to grab hold
Of the trunk of the hollow sycamore

On the bank. For a moment, it looked at me,
And I stared back, its claws dug into the tree

Bark, not with hostility, but as in embracing
The familiarity of its home, before ascending

Into the top of the trunk's empty cavern—
The sound of the brook's rush merging with

The sunlight flashing over the frigid water,
Clouds of my breath steaming the frosty air.

Satori

for Robert Jones

Yes, it has been long enough. It has been long enough that hearing
from you this evening is much like having stepped onto what is

apparently an unfamiliar subway car, and in a moment of the terrific
velocity of G-force, I find myself, years later, sitting at my worktable

here in my studio near the foot of Long Mountain in South Amherst,
Massachusetts, writing you. I especially appreciate your emailing

the photograph of you standing beside Robert Spiess, who is wearing
the medal from his having been presented with the Shiki Award,

and holding open the bound citation in his hands. You are correct
in your assessment that he was in league with Emerson and Mencken,

as an editor. Anyone can see what the award meant to him by
his facial expression and body language. Did you know that he was

a surrogate father to me? Thank you for the update on your Lavelle
translations—I appreciate that. Louis Lavelle being the Christian

mystic of the *intelligentsia,* in direct opposition to existentialism.
The Act of Presence is a text I look forward to rereading. Could it be
    that

I remember studying Lavelle all those years ago? I feel that, through
you, the universe touched me on the shoulder this evening, and I am

grateful that you precipitated my own *presence* in a deeply-experienced
satorial flash—just in an instant. D. T. Suzuki wrote: *Satori is the
    raison*

d'être of Zen, without which Zen is no Zen. You reminded me of the
    truth
of who I am, where my eternal home is, here or elsewhere: *in the
    moment.*

Vixen

Here on the farm the vixen
       hunts during the day; how
              exquisitely she moves, how beautifully

fox-red, whenever she breaks off
       the language of her body that intends
              never to be seen. Last Sunday, I crossed

over to the windbreak
       of leafless trees, among the hummocks
              that descend into the drainage ditch beyond

where she was tracking,
       unaware of my immediacy, within a few
              yards, so mindful was she of mice, of rats

in the matted stalks of the meadow.
       This afternoon, she emerged
              in the clearing beyond the barn. I watched

her stretch and shake
       luxuriously, so unconstrained
              after a day and night of winter rain. Now,

she begins to trail
       a new scent, nose down
              among the dark roots of the browned grass.

Sinewed, she articulates open
       ground on black-furred feet—
              a streak of flame igniting the wind, a mind

at one in the conflagration
       of the moment, shoulders
              hunched, arched hair on neck, her vernacular

perpetual patrol
     and reconnaissance,
         her sudden disappearance only an exhibition

of her sudden reappearance,
     her reappearance the command parlance
         of her disguise among what is apparent in

her inexorable leap,
     pouncing on a meadow vole,
         or whatever stirs beneath her, as our hearts

quicken, her saliva-flecked tongue
     flashing, the tail of her succulent prey
         brandished between the wedge of her jaws.

Visitation

A year after my mother's death, I stood on the front porch
of the second story flat in Ansonia, a Connecticut factory town.

I was drawn to a box of my mother's things.
Among them, a folio-sized book of Edward Curtis photographs.

Upon opening the volume, I was mesmerized
by the sepia portraits of Native Americans. Deeply entranced,

after some time, and especially as when one finally realizes
that you are being watched, I looked up—the image of mother

standing beside me. She was not at all in flesh, and it was not
what paranormal experts might call an ectoplasmic appearance,

but somewhere in between. I felt comforted
by mother's presence, young enough, at nine, not to think

this was something unusual. The message mother conveyed was
that she wanted me to make books central to my life.

Wordlessly, she informed me.
The visitation may be all of the poems that I have written.

Etched

We dispel the notion
that poems can be tossed off,

that there are tricks
to jump-starting their success,

that there are any number
of ways to achieve

lasting resonance
within them. We portend

that poetry is written
with similar intent

as the lines that are etched
across the palms of our hands.

In the Shade of a Cave

We hike halfway up Mount Toby to where the gorge drops
off and takes the thin stream of Roaring Brook down

toward the culvert beneath train tracks to Cranberry Pond.
I explain that the water is normally roaring every spring

from the snowmelt; however, not having much of a winter
has affected the watersheds. I illustrate that usually

the force of the brook hammers the stones, that the sound
mixes with the ionization of the water rising above the cliffs,

so that you can see, hear, and smell the torrent all at once.
In giving Bob a guided tour of the flora bordering the trail

this mid-April, I find the Quaker Ladies grouped in blue
and white clusters at the bottom, in the scrub meadow that

overlooks the pond. Farther up where I warn him
that here is where the trail begins to become steep, I spot

one nodding purple trillium, then point out the others
blazing their own trail up the slope. He aims the camera

to shoot his photographs of what he describes
as their flowers *looking downward,* and I explain that is why

part of their name includes the word *nodding.* He tells me
that he was an infantryman in the Battle of the Bulge,

one of four soldiers out of a platoon of forty who survived
the surging stormtroopers. I point to the bright yellow

discs of inflorescence of coltsfoot flourishing beside
a trickle of a stream cutting its way through the black mud.

There! I exclaim, and identify the four-lobed lush purple
flowers of hepatica, whose royal hues can be easily missed

due to their diminutive size among leaf litter. I speak
with an intended ebullient clarity that I hope he remembers

when we find the clearing beneath the mossy cliffs halfway
up the mountain, speckled white with the luscious

blossoming of bloodroot. I inform him that there is only
a two-week window of our seeing this perennial in the wild,

of which he shows his rapt appreciation by taking one
photograph after another. *Do you see that one,* I say, placing

one of his hands in one of mine, as I draw a straight line
to where one bloodroot flower grows in the shade of a cave

in the cliffs. *Oh, I see*, he answers, then continues:
Yesterday I couldn't feel my hands and feet from the trench foot I got

in the battle. They only gave us thin gloves, so we could fire our rifles.
My feet froze, since the boots they gave us were not much,

and the socks were too goddamn thin! We look at each other,
with mutual understanding beneath green cliffs, whose

natural architecture we both admire, among blossoms
of bloodroot that star the entire vertical rise in the sunlight.

Dream of Judita Vaiciunaite

for Jonas Zdanys

In the dream, she arranges to meet me aboard the cutter.
Our hair streams in the wind, and I ask her about the women

Sitting upon the rocks of the harbor, and standing among
The stony cliffs along the shore, all singing in the polyphony

Of Hildegaard von Bingen, and she informs me that
They protect the city, that they turn away the ships of enemies

And guide the vessels of its friends. Then I ask her about
The ranks of men harvesting the ripe coastal grass for haying,

And she answers me that this is one example how husbandry
Is inculcated into the society, that in another life

Many of the men seen harvesting were proponents
Of selfish means, who favored plundering the earth for profit

Instead of managing the balance of her natural ways.
Aboard the cutter in the dream with the wind in our hair,

She speaks a poem about wreathing a rainbow in the sky
On the day before she died, after a night of heavy rain,

In the book that glows with the images of her beloved Vilnius,
After I turn out the light on the night table, her poems page

Through my mind with the icons of their images of wild
Chamomile, plum blossoms, and bitterns contained

In the lyrics. Dandelion honey, the red of the autumn sage,
The mother-of-pearl clouds about to vanish from the sky

Like the great wings of the sea eagle, who is no longer lonely;
And as dusk is extinguished on its wings, her white hair

Changes again into the black hair of her youth, as I awaken
From the dream with the sound of the cutter still in my ears.

Cameltoes

To dress with such a flare is to parade what is
only barely masked, and to brazenly unmask

the power of the feminine, but, when perpetrated
in a manner as this, is evincing the third chakra

force of power over another: the enforced
unmitigated swagger, whether petite or bodacious,

that mandates more than a sideward
look, is not so much an advertisement for itself

but more of a dare, which, if it is then not taken,
intends to weaken those who practice the remnant

social skills of the modest, and to disarm
those who openly gawk by disabling whatever

their intentions are by either leading them
by the chains of their own lust, and by disabusing

them in dissing the attention that they draw;
or worse, by unleashing the wrath of Diana

anytime an unsuspecting Acteon may cast
an awkward glance her way, upon which, she will

find this as reason enough to take the opportunity
to turn him into the stag that he most surely

will become, only to be humiliated, to be hunted
down, and to be torn apart by the raging hounds.

The Dante Alighieri Summer *Paradiso Al Fresco*

It is not yet your vacation, but it could be—
The day being so perfectly lit beneath

The high cerulean sky, dotted with cumulus;
The air so fresh after days of June rain.

You decide to take out the leftover spinach
Pasta and white clam sauce from the refrigerator;

Dust it generously with *Parmesan-Romano-Asiago,*
Rotate several full turns of black pepper

From the wooden grinder, and drizzle a couple
Of tablespoons of virgin olive oil over all of that.

You have worked your way through all the levels
Of hell: the job, your boss, an irascible partner,

And then persevered through all seven
Of the purgatorial circles, much described

By that beloved flirt, Saint Theresa of Avila,
Who it is said levitated several times in the galley

Kitchen of the nunnery to the extent that
Her fellow sisters needed to pull her by her habit

Back down to the ground. By now you can use
A respite in paradise, although a half hour would

Do; besides, where you find yourself now
Appears to be the Florian, a sidewalk café, with

The most fascinating of angelic faces at each table.
In your abandon, you order the side salad to go

With the pasta, which is simply called the *Al Fresco*,
Combining chick peas, cucumber, and Vidalia onion

In Tahini dressing. When the waitress
Takes your order, you don't notice the size

Of her wings until she turns to go; and before
You can speak the thought, she turns back around

And suggests a drink that she believes best to
Accompany your meal. As you take another sip

Of the iced cherry juice with orange seltzer,
You notice the trio sitting at the table next to you.

Proffering his violin as the sacred object that it is,
Is Vivaldi; then beside him, Dante is sharing

Photographs of himself and Beatrice, taken
On their vacation in the Pyrenees, to Botticelli,

Who is sitting in front of a plate full of empty
Shells from his abundant appetizer of clams casino—

All three originals beaming in the verisimilitude
Of their specific and inimitable perfections,

All seated beneath a sword of light the Archangel
Gabriel is holding above them like a torch of flame.

The Young Woman

Wearing a burgundy summer dress
with straps and a pair of white pumps

with open heels and toes, she is crossing
the four-way intersection

at the traffic light; waits momentarily—
then crosses the highway, delightfully

insouciant. If her long legs could possibly
idealize themselves, they would; since

they are nothing less than beautiful, but
they do not, nor do I, because she would be

offended by such comparisons;
and since women of any age prefer

to be seen just as they are, emblematic
of their own beauty and mystery, without

 idealization. Although, the angels
of her shoulder blades appear to nearly

smile at me, as her arms swing as she walks.
Perhaps, this is because I never quite see

her face, as the straps of her dress
dangle and bounce across her upper back,

whose smooth tanned skin any man
would find sacred, with or without the use

of a lexicon or a map; since words cannot
describe it, and searching for them would be

as feckless as trying to describe it. After
she has crossed the highway with such

unconscious elan, she begins to walk
toward the malls; and as she does so,

she flips a part of the shoulder-length hair
that has been swept into her face,

a signature gesture that reveals more about
her being in rhythm with herself,

and with life itself, than any personal trait
about her, individually, since she moves

around whatever obstacle that she discerns
is in her way; as easily as stepping lightly

over stones leading across a body
of water; as simply as she might be stepping

across the water and seeing her own face
reflected there amid the stones;

as instinctively, and in such harmony,
that upon her leaving, we, too, now see

the light shine in the rippled water
where the image of her face had been.

Incident at Eel River

I maintain my balance just before
    I would have slid over the stones,
        rolling with the ones I kicked downhill, and flash back

to my time, as a young man, on the banks
    of the Eel River, north of Eureka, California.
        I remember feeling fortunate then, too, to find stones

to guide me where I crossed to sandy
    shoals on the other shore; recall the quiet
        on that side, far enough away from the late night traffic

on the highway, of tires spinning
    on asphalt that the distance muffled;
        the light of a sky full of stars sparkling in the water, as

I untied my sleeping bag, climbed in,
    closed my eyes. Hours later, that I speculate
        was the dead zone, 3:00 a.m., I awakened to an animal

brushing its muzzle against my head, protruding out
    of the sleeping bag. Whatever it was huffed in gasps—
        nudging and snorting, snorting and nudging. Although

I read of this phenomena, I never
    experienced being *frozen with fear*. I tried to move—
        my arms and legs wouldn't respond; opened my mouth,

but the genesis of a roar that roiled
    in the vortex of my solar plexus wouldn't erupt
        into the careening sound of malaise. I lay there, unable

to release my catharsis of horror,
    my fear of whatever animal had inspected this
        intruder in the wilderness of its domain. When I thought

that the beast had departed, felt
>the lockdown of my body loosen, the lockjaw
>>slacken, and then with the static energy regenerating
>>>itself,

let loose the roar that must have
>shaken the surface of the Eel River;
>>the roar frightening the birds beginning to sing; the roar

that may have even alarmed
>whatever animal it was who thrust its muzzle into
>>the top of my head, whose tracks in the sand of the shoal

in the early morning were indecipherable
>as unmistakable as was my decision to gather
>>my sleeping bag and retrace my steps over the stones
>>>along

the shallows, to scale back up
>the bank to the highway, where, at
>>the time, I was in a terrible hurry to commence with my
>>>life.

The Scent

I came upon the body of a dead raccoon among
The furze, its grimace frozen beside the ice-sheathed

Brook. The way in which its body lay contorted
On the ice crust caused me to think it may have fallen

From an overhanging branch, as I bent, keeping
A safe distance. Later, on the walk in front

Of the house, I felt the housecat, the one who always
Wanted to go out, and once out, wanted back in,

Brushing against my trousers, and looked down,
Only to match gazes with the raccoon who had taken

Refuge in the neighbors' carriage house next door.
It must have smelled the scent of the body

Of the dead raccoon on me, possibly sensing I might
Be one of its larger unmasked brethren; and since

I wasn't sure if it were rabid, I stamped one foot
Twice, to spook it away from its rubbing against me.

I could see from the quizzical look of its eyes
That it was unsure why I was dissuading it from

Continuing its spooning, then it bolted, making its
Way through the space beneath the fence separating

The neighbor's yard from ours, looking behind
At me all the while, the click of its paws echoing

Over the salt-stained asphalt, as it slipped back into
Its own mystery of being, of itself as raccoon,

Returning to the icy darkness of the winter night.
Months later, early one summer morning, I saw it

Flicking its tail, both sentry and thief, perched
Atop a telephone pole, peering down on me.

Homage to Ed Ricketts

When you drove up Drake Avenue that evening, you had
Just spoken with your sister Alice over the phone.

Your last words to her being, *I have never been any happier*
In my entire life. You had just married a young woman,

You were only days away from leaving on another
Expedition to the Queen Charlotte Islands with Steinbeck

To write a book that was to be entitled *The Outer Shores.*
Was it your musing about the sea worm that distracted you?

Or was it the list of what you needed to pack
For the expedition? Did the rusted 1936 Packard stall

On the railroad tracks, as the Delmonte Express, on its way
From San Francisco, turned the blind curve from behind

One of the canneries, to bear down on you, as the engineer
Blew the whistle several times, before the train crashed

Into the car, carrying you down the tracks three hundred
Feet away, spilling you and the Packard off to the side?

The collision startled most of the saintly bums from
Their dreams at the foot of the hill along Cannery Row.

At that moment, Monterey would never be any quieter.
Nothing would ever be quite the same again.

John Steinbeck's Doc and Joseph Campbell's *Hero with*
A Thousand Faces would pass from this specific incarnation

Three days short of your fifty-first birthday. Described as
Having a face that was *part Christ, part satyr,* the wise voice

That everyone seemed to listen to was silenced because
Of either a stalled car or the distraction of your thinking

About the ecology of sardines, instead of paying attention
To an oncoming passenger train crossing an intersection

Without the safety of a wigwag. I imagine that you reside
In your own version of paradise: dawn at low tide on one

Of the most remote of the Queen Charlotte's, off the coast
Of British Columbia, the tidal flats spread out before you

For your prospecting of marine specimens, stretching out
In the bracing cold and the pink brightness of the new day—

The innumerable starfish dotting their universe over
The expanse of the abated Pacific tide, and you persevering

In the perpetuity of the perigee and the apogee in gathering
Nothing but grace from the abundance of the sea.

Prescience

Afternoon pillars of sunlight
        angled from the west windows
               and touched the book of myths I had placed

back on the shelf. The image of Pandora
        and her ill-fated box still hovering
               in the air. I remembered the several pages

I composed on a similar afternoon
        backlit by sunlight, of what appeared
               to be penciled hieroglyphic scrawl from an

Egyptian incarnation.
        Continuing to stand, mesmerized by
               the perpetuating image of Pandora, beside

the set of encyclopedia my mother
        had purchased, despite my father's
               strong disapproval, for a boy of five, I was

transfixed by the imitation gilt
        and red leatherette bindings. However,
               my mouth formed the letter, and sounded

O, as if I were Pandora, and all
        of the grim spirits, instead of ills that
               would plague the world, which she released

from the dreaded box, paralleled
        my entering this life, one in which
               I knew I had sacred contracts with those in

previous lives, and even though
        I saw myself years in the future,
               as a writer, I also nearly recognized, as did

Pandora, the faces of those
      with whom both she and I
            would attempt to make reparation with, and

those who remained
      faceless with whom I
            was to reconcile, one of my hands touching

the book's binding, as I stood,
      with the past, present, and future
            streaming among dust motes in the sunlight.

The Blind

Walking back from the mailbox on the roadside,
With junk mail in my hands, I think about

All of the letters from Catholic societies that
Were addressed to my mother after she died.

The letters often contained pendants devoted to
The Blessed Virgin, and all of them, I am sure,

Were petitions for donations. My response,
As a child, was: *Why didn't all of these people*

Know that my mother had died, why were they
Still sending her letters? Receiving those letters

Reminded me of the grief I would feel when
The blind would ring the buzzer on the front

Steps of our home, their stark white canes
Made only more isolate in the brightness

Of the sun. The blind would go door to door
To sell packets of needles, and I would always

Be startled by the obviousness of their loss,
The bleak unlit hallways their lives had become.

I recall one blind woman, with a spectrally
Beautiful face, whose pupils were occluded

With a milkiness, whom my mother purchased
Needles from, my mother the seamstress who

Could have provided the blind woman with
Sewing kits full of needles. A similar grief

Resonated within me when, after waiting for
The door to open, I was told that you weren't

In today, the stab of disappointment an arrow
Slowly quivering in me, despite my denials.

Being bereft is never censure to the heart
Opening, it is central to it, it is the key.

Things I Know I Love

First, it was seeing the fresh sweet corn
        placed in rows of high stacks around
                the stand that a South Amherst neighbor keeps on

her front lawn; and this then led
        to my thinking about the one celebratory
                meal I savor every summer, which is mussels and

sweet corn salad. So, I selected
        a half dozen ears of corn, and brought
                them home, to which I added certain ingredients

to, after I boiled the ears: white pinto
        beans; sweet onion; freshly squeezed
                lemon; chili powder, to which I drizzled a mixture

of olive oil and balsamic over
        the fresh mussels that I added—
                the poor man's, or the everyman's, fruit of the sea.

What punctuated my concluding
        the preparation of the salad, which I
                placed into the refrigerator to chill, that I will savor

for several dinners, with
        a glass of an affordable Bordeaux, was
                my listening to Mozart's *Linz Symphony*. The music,

is one of lavish
        abandon and of proclamation.
                If Mozart loved anything, and he loved many things;

he loved his wife,
        Constanze; and he had a fancy for expensive
                shoes, as I might love summer and my celebrating it

by listening to
>   his composition, which Mozart
>   dedicated to the citizens of Linz; and after being

bathed in my own joy
>   I have created what is
>   symphonic, in a gustatory and culinary tribute to

summer, with a salad
>   of delectable mussels
>   and dewy-eared sweet corn, to share with friends.

The Snake

Beauty as sinuousness: more than
a foot long; alternate yellow

and brown stripes running the length
of its body, ending in a pointed

black tail. When I needed to walk
past to go to the barn with

my recycling, it didn't move. I was
close enough to bend down to place

it in my hands. Although I was sure
it wouldn't have enjoyed that, so

I didn't. You would have appreciated
being there with me for that moment:

its head poised about five or six
inches off the ground in a right angle

to its body. It was so comfortable
with me that I even walked past it

again on my way to the mail box
on the road. And there it was, head

held high, body curled in fashionable
loops, that were in keeping with

the ease of my interaction with its
primed electric elegance, its watchful

stillness, the penetrating incisiveness
of the dots of its bulging black eyes.

By the time I was back with my mail,
it was gone.

Apples

When I serve one of the apples I bought
On a white plate, sliced in quarters, then

Sliced again in thirds, along with a slice
Of cheese, it is an elegant meal unto itself,

Not necessarily breakfast, but a spare lunch,
With that always attractive combination

Of aesthetics and utility. The apples I chose
For this week were Cortlands, Macouns,

And Honey Crisps, each its own cadenza
In the symphony of streaming October

Sunlight, as strong as the light in Emmaus
When Christ reappeared to the disbelief

Of his apostles. Each apple, one for each
Day, as resilient as if it were its own last

Meal, as if we could ever plan a more perfect,
More impeccable last meal. The apples

I chose offered their own salient characteristics,
Such as the robustness of the Cortland, and

The crunch of the Macoun, and the sweetness
Of the Honey Crisp. Each bite its own taste

And texture. Each its own compliment
To the steady inflorescence of the October

Sunlight, with the sense of ending and
Beginning, with the aspect of the light of Christ

Already in our heart, with that heady fullness
Of our brimming over with the abundance

Of the fruit of the harvest, and in what is
The redolence of the fragrance of apples.

In Memory of Jack Gilbert

In my passing the herd of goats grazing the meadow
Adjacent to Little Creek Farm, I think of you, especially

In my seeing the male with his twisted horns crowning
His wizened head, the sunlight flickering between

The birches and the pines this morning as I drive north.
The baritone of the semis passing me going south with

Their diesel engines droning in the bluster of the wind
Shear as they blow by me. I compare your work to itself

As I compare Mozart's *Prague Symphony* driving up
To Petersham and then to his *Jupiter Symphony* driving

Back to Amherst. As you might write, the achievement
Is in the achieving, in the delight of eating the apple past

The seeds and the core, in loving a woman beyond
One's magisterial heart to find what it might be that draws

Us into deeper mystery when we move past ego
And adoration to the essence that is even further past

Lust and beauty. On our last hike together before you left
Fort Juniper to travel to your Greek mountain,

I joked about the plethora of mushrooms, newly sprouted
After the late summer rain, and how they were

Yet to be fully formed, reminding me of early drafts
Of poems, and you laughed. You possessed the wisdom

To teach gently, then fiercely; and to discern the difference
Between the two. With you now irrevocably gone,

I envision you prospering on your own hardscrabble island
Much like Prospero, the wind in your hair on a cliff above

The bright blue of the Aegean. Although your books will
Never be buried, at least not by you or those who have been

Nourished by them. Although what you might now hear,
Among the island's stony silences, may just sound similar

To the applause Prospero heard, in the cadence of waves
Crashing on the shore, releasing you from the bonds

Of the rigor of your own poems, which you so obstinately
Held to; of their ardor, which you offered to us as gifts;

As beacons in the night, in whose distant glow we steer
Toward, when each one of us dips the oars and begins

To row, headed for our own remote island, upon which
All the years of sorrow will be worth the yearning

Of our particular heart, for whatever reasons, that we will
Later discover, are why, at last, we have come.

Asking

for Elainie Lillios

I would never capitulate, even for you;
Even more so, especially not for you.

There is such an ever present Eros
And spirituality in the alchemy between us.

So, there isn't room for capitulation,
Just because I might want to please you.

The work of music and words was done
With respect to itself, and my attempt

In creating within a collaboration, which
Is probably one of the most difficult

Challenges and possible achievements,
To accomplish. I appreciate what you

Did with what I provided you with.
I think the lines regarding the moonlight

And the dusting of snow did deserve to be
Cut. How you arranged the sequence,

Seasonally, from what I provided,
Is a testament to your working with me,

And I with you. Also, I believe I opened
The door for you to *ask for it all.*

It is salient, when a woman does that,
And, as a man, one can stand fast,

In accommodating her request, and he
Pleases her. *Asking for it all* is significant,

Only because the woman who asks for it
Trusts enough to, as you do, with grace.

Windhorse

Slabs of white marble in stacks,
the pictographs carved in them,

then finding this thin tablet.
My hands running across the intaglio

of a frieze; its smoothness to touch,
the celebration of *Bacchus* in honor

of *Equus*—
unearthing the actual vision of it

in the archeology of dream;
the going to and the digging through

layers of consciousness, as in layers
of earth

in the city of *Equestrium*.
That is what I heard. The word spoken

as it was spoken.
Workers and trainers

moving here and there, as in a kind
of bas-relief.

Then someone speaking
to me, instructing me with the urgency

in their stentorian voice.
Although I did not

necessarily know the language.
Then the muscular flanks shining—

a chiseled kind of strength;
the natural aesthetic of the uncut mane,

the sheer beauty of it.
Then putting my foot in the boot

of the narrow stirrup,
I inhaled the fragrance of the leather

before hearing it creak with my weight,
and I settled into the saddle

on the breadth of its massive back.
Before I could even think, the wind

in my hair, the mane flying.
Ride, he said, and I did,

in the timeless instant
before waking again into this life.

Green Olives

I stood at the crest of the hill on the rock wall among
Stakes of barbed wire fence looking down at the cows

That grazed the rolling hillocks overlooking the city
Below, and remarked, *What abandon, what freedom.*

My friend, Darrell, responded, *You poet!* This was
The first time I had run away from home, from being

Locked out of the house for not wearing the ill-fitting
Wide wale corduroys. This was before I ran away

And acquired my first apartment, with an over-the-road
Truck driver who snored, when I was sixteen.

This was before I inadvertently broke the storm window
Of the screen door when I slammed it as I left for

My commute to morning classes of my freshman year
At college; both my father and stepmother continuing

To throw cups, plates, and their breakfast against
The dining room wall. This was before I returned

In the evening to policemen who arrested me
For breach of peace, before I spent the night in jail,

Before I had dropped out of school. When
I stood there at the crest of the hill, the entire world

Appeared to be spread out before me. Then Darrell
And I descended to the bottom to the white farm house

Where his grandmother lived. He told me she would
Make us lunch, and that his favorite part of lunch were

79

The green olives. We were served bologna sandwiches
With yellow mustard on white bread. Then Darrell's

Grandmother placed a whole jar of green olives stuffed
With pimento beside our two glasses of milk. I can still

Hear Darrell chew his sandwich with gusto, as I did mine;
And we consumed one olive, then a second, and another,

Until most of the jar had been emptied. *Finish the rest,*
Darrell's grandmother urged, solicitously, the green olives

Tasting like *abandon* and *freedom*. Their succulence
Complimenting a common lunch. Tonight, when I wake

I think of the green olives, flecked with red pepper flakes,
That I have in the refrigerator, and can nearly taste them,

Their lush pungence blossoming across my palate,
And think about the wild abandon of Gorky's street urchins

In *My Childhood*. I think about making a running break
Past the grazing cows along the hillocks of the slope

Of that verdant hill, and coming to know the taste
Of green olives and how they open out across the tongue,

Filling the mouth with the nascence of language,
That led me to feast on untold meals of freedom and song.

Flowering

For three days that April,
      we followed the trail
           up to a green meadow—

its deep color lush after
      the winter rains; and sitting
           among the California poppies,

that studded the grasses
      with an orange pointillism,
           a young blonde woman sat,

wearing nothing but
      hiking boots, her pack
           beside her, amid that flowering.

We stopped and spoke
      in a casual demeanor, but
           as in the myth of the divine

feminine, in which she
      challenged the male gods,
           who had just happened upon

her, in moving
      the feather she had placed
           in the air between them, and,

no matter how
      hard they blew their
           breath, they were powerless

in their being able
      to even touch it,
           there was a similar element

of the unmovable
      among each of us,
            an aspect of gravity that kept

us apart, but
      brought us together
            by the magnetizing force

of the allure of her body,
      of that astonishment,
            as she sat, enthroned, on

the sloping hillside
      of orange poppies,
            sunbathing in her boots.

Mary Oliver

My memory of her is as evanescent
        as the light bulb camera flash
                of a Stieglitz portrait of O'Keeffe.

The image that remains with me
        is that I furtively studied her face,
                the quietude of its naked sensuality,

the way you feel the self-conscious
        trembling of a spotted doe
                when you have entered the meadow

where she is browsing, or the sight
        of the of bearded mussels that
                disappear and then reappear along

the stone quay reaching out into
        the sea, in rhythm with your doubt
                that you may have seen them from

afar, and the vision of them between
        the white-capped surf, that reaffirms
                their existence, washing over their

iridescence again.
        After having walked into
                the bookstore she was working in

on Commercial Street in Provincetown,
        what I noticed more than anything
                was her stillness those thirty-five

years ago, as I browsed
        the poetry section, occasionally
                looking around, and sometimes

between, the shelves of the rows
      of books, as fluidly arranged as
            the shells among the stones found

along the sand of the beach.
      There she sat, behind the counter—
            mist draping the cobblestones

of the street, the sound
      of the tide beating time on the shore.
            Her living presence made me think

of Vermeer's *Girl with a Pearl*
      Earring, although she didn't even
            require any adornment jewelry

would have diminished
      the radiance of, as she breathed into
            the study of quiet that she became.

Rilkean Dream

I dreamed of myself as a light following
A greater series of lights, in a particular
Pattern of circles—

A veritable sense of a spiritual
Architecture, as in the shell of a conch,
Or what is sonic in the soaring arcs

Of language—
What Rilke's monk exhibits
In his painting—

Brushing the luminous colors
Of the ineffable in words.
Transcendence isn't tangible, or tacit,

But a glimmering,
As a ray of light, or the single wave
In one ripple of water after another.

The Knowing

What has awakened you is not
So much the headlights of your

Neighbor's car illuminating the walls
Of the room at 2:00 a.m. as much

As the cold hard rain from the violent
Thunderstorm that probably destroyed

The flower heads of the purple
And yellow flags of the iris, unaware

Of their nobility, after only a day
They began blooming. The present

Moment is more of that, the knowing
Of that moment deeply, and then

Remembering what you saw on the face
Of your friend, how she acted like a deer

Ready to bolt across a meadow
She couldn't run fast enough to traverse

Because the malevolent actions
Of many who live in this world are

Too much to bear. The present moment
Remains. It is all we ever have, and in it,

We inherit everything, a container that
Holds all and nothing, always becoming,

Transforming itself into being from
This to something less and then

Something more; as the rain starts again,
Falling harder, the lightning flashing

Across the dark sky, yellow streaks
Flaring in the purple petals of the iris.

The Order of Things
In Memory of Robert Winne

1.

One pink-red rose among rosettes
Blooms beside the flickering prismatic
Spider webs strung among the florescence
Of yarrow and mint leaves,
Where we stood last autumn
When you were still alive,
This brilliant June morning; birdsong rising
From the sheen of the needles of hemlock
Branches along the path.

2.

Purple flags of wild iris
And the large yellow buttons of the corollas
Of oxeye daisies thrive among foxtail grass
Amid the *ahness* of a single flower head
Of orange hawkweed; one whole shoulder
Of the trail up to the Peace Pagoda
Bursting white with mountain laurel;
Some of their flower clusters
Shattered after the heavy June rains
And scattered beneath their shrubbery
In the detritus of leaves and dried mud.

3.

The sound of a woodpecker
Rapping on a tree trunk, then stopping,
And rapping again, echoes from afar,
Deeper in the woods. An entire plywood
Platform of stone sculptures near the crest
Of the last hill are still largely intact, most
Of which have survived the wind and the rain,
Since the last time we walked here.

4.

When I reach the top of the trail
To the open field before the Peace Pagoda,
A mourning cloak circles me several times;
Frogs croak from the Koi pond; a whir
Of electric hand tools buzzes
From workers in the meditation hall,
That much closer to being fully constructed;
The stone lion dooryard guardians,
That we saw being erected on their brick
Dais and plinth, now perennially welcome
The sangha who enter in all of their Shambhala
Strength; images of Avalokiteśvara adorn
Either side of the carved wooden temple
Doors; someone has moved the bench
We would sit on into the small meadow
And placed it farther into the shade.

5.

Pink mountain laurel compliments the color
Of the pond lilies just opening across the water.
Yellow iris blooms among purple clover,
Vetch, and ragged robin.
Fallen white peonies and desiccated rugosa roses
Lay collapsed in the grass or rock in the breeze
That ripples the lines of multi-colored
Prayer flags over the pond
Where the diphthong of one frog answers
The elasticity in the voice of another.

6.

The redness of a Japanese maple shades
The entrance beside a boulder
To the path encircling the pond, but
Does not cover the space left by your absence.

Bumblebees pollinate a stand of phlox,
Their chartreuse petals exclamatory among
The small green fronds of meadow grass;
The diaphanous wings of mating dragonflies,
When they collide, sizzle
Against each other, instantaneously.

7.

When I look deeply into the yellow center
Of the open white pond lily,
It is as if I gaze directly into myself.
Gray-black tadpoles and orange Koi
Skitter through the pond water
When my shadow moves along the shore;
A water snake slithers across
The pond's surface, its head disappearing
Among the cattails and reeds before
The exaggerated cursives of its body.

8.

The first prayer flag on one of the lines
Snaps in a gust, well before the others.
A grouse drums in the birch woods.
A tiger swallowtail flies up and out
Of the petaled shade of the dogwood's
Custard-colored blossoms,
Just beyond the reclining Buddha
In the north niche, the one that
Is said to be entering Parinirvana.

9.

After I circumnavigate the Peace Pagoda,
I find there is nowhere to go,
And that you are one now
With the nothingness that is your home

And will be ours.
Birch leaves rustle in the slightest breeze.
Sunlit patches of stellaria brighten in the grass.
All of this has not happened quite this way
Before; all of this, despite its recurrence,
Will not ever be this way again.

Daylilies

When I left this morning,
      under a deep cerulean sky,
            the orange daylilies were thronging

the mailbox beside
      the road, petals still
            closed, beaded with droplets of dew;

so much green in the grass, in the trees,
      the sunlight streaking everything,
            making all sparkle, infusing every color

with shades of gold and yellow.
      When I returned just before noon,
            the daylilies had opened their supple

orange mouths,
      tasting the air, savoring the breeze
            with tongues of anther and pistil;

the chiffon of their
      throats offered the coolness
            of song and practical shade and nectar

for a pollinating bee.
      They hold as much
            gladness as we can imagine, filling us

with orange rapture,
      the orange of daylilies,
            rising on stems by the roadside farm;

the lithe cups of their mouths,
      spilling over with urgency,
            with exultation, unfolded and full,

blooming with heedless
     abandon, with pleasures
         so tantalizing they invite us to look,

to breathe the diligence
     of their color, to be as bedazzled
         as they at the pinnacle of their lives.

A Way of Seeing

When I saw the first
    monarch of mid-summer,
        so transfixed was I by its dark orange wings,

I hesitated for what may
    have been an eternal instant, when
        I said aloud, *Monarch*, and it flew around me,

as it might around a milkweed
    pod, although the milkweed has
        not quite ripened here in mid-July. It floated

around me like a friend,
    an ally; it settled on the ground, to display its
        wings, fanning them open, fanning them closed,

then leaving them unfolded,
    to reveal the small finger-length of black
        thorax and abdomen, the white spots bejeweling

the black rims of its wings
    that divide the lush orange,
        as if they were panes of stained glass, fanned

and fanned again,
    as if to say, *How well made; how*
        orange my wings that migrate south thousands of
            miles;

or maybe I spoke
    those words aloud, no matter;
        because, when I moved, the monarch rose up,

and sauntered across
    summer air. I stopped, breathed in
        a reminder of the morning, a brightness and

fulfillment vanishing;
      endangered and soon extinct, as
            when we look and see, there in the empty air.

Summer Rain

Its patter is distinguished, its rhythm
Pools then pools within itself again.

It is the slow, persistent music of lovers
Who are at one in making their gazing

At God last long after their lovemaking
Is over. Just by the look on their faces,

The divine afterglow of their union
Is deepened by the mesmerizing

And seductive healing of the slow-falling
Nature of its meditative tympani.

It is the Paris of weather phenomena.
Who wouldn't imagine themselves

In the arms of their soul mate just by
The softness and rustle of its sound?

It is the freshness of the newly opened
Flowers of iris and peony nodding

To the beat in the coolness of its
Falling, sometimes a petal loosening

And dropping into a puddle in
The garden that is alive with its wetness.

Mint

Mist rises from the ridge
        of Long Mountain after the thunderous
                morning rains. By noon the heat has swept

away the coolness lavished
        by the storms. Walking beside the thicket,
                the fragrance of mint permeates the air with

such a deep pungence of herbal
        earth that its rich odor could be a color,
                such as yellow, and that its perfume is of such

an effect that it possesses
        a brightness that becomes enflamed
                in the rising heat of the day. That the mint

had been cut back to provide
        a view of the traffic passing on the road,
                it is similar to what forgiveness may be, in that

after mint is cut its fragrance
        suffuses the very air we breathe;
                that the smell might adhere to our clothes,

and certainly instills the redolence
        of it in our memory, is specific
                to the act of the mint being sheared, or what

act initiated the necessity
        of forgiveness, which then lead to the balm
                that we may think of being a comforting tea.

Only if we were more
        akin to mint itself could we
                release such an essence, and so immediately;

although the mint could prove
      to us a salient lesson, one
            that would be easy to remember, to attest by,

if by any slander, or insult,
      even great offense, that has cut us,
            to recall how the oils of mint are released

when their stems are rendered, and what
      richness in healing pervades the nostrils of
            all those who are fortunate to just inhale.

The Snail

It isn't in reaching the crest
    of the rise of the gorge
        and already wading in the sound

of the rush of the brook.
    Nor is it in standing above
        the flume just before the waterfall

and watching the lacy
    stream flow over its bed,
        flecked with white quartz below

its ripples. Neither
    is it in pausing
        to watch the snake pour its ribbons

over the dirt and
    the stones on the path.
        All of that gives its own reason for

awakening within,
    with a plentitude
        of spirit, but it is in seeing the snail

in a streak of sunlight
    falling in a band across
        the trail, in a plank of light. It is in

seeing this snail's spiral
    mollusk shell, its pink Lilliputian
        face and black-tipped horns rising

to meet your face as
    you look down toward its
        glistening body, lavished in its own

viscosity, in the dew,
       in the golden light of the sun.
              It is this miracle that you will carry

with you as does
       the snail its earth house shell
              wherever you will go, always

remembering the spiral
       emblem leading within
              itself and out of itself in such

a fluid and harmonic
       fashion, whose circular
              design is an image of the divine.

The Treadle and the Light

The spirit is the treadle, often with a foot to the floor
Making up for lost time. The soul is the memory

Of the last time you saw your mother happy, while
Picnicking with you and a friend of hers

From New Jersey, on a beach in Miami, two weeks
Before she died after walking you to school

On the first day of third grade, only a week after
Having arrived with your father in a move north

To New England, where she thought you would have
A better life. The soul is what you have seen

In the face of your lover. It is the light that floods out
Of the face of the one woman you have loved

In your life, whose radiance fills you, then fills you
Again, and in whom you find what is oceanic.

It is what you discover in the brimming and singing,
And the singing and brimming in that. The spirit is

The feeling of the push and pull of our oars
In the water; how the strokes of our favorite pen

Sound, scratching across a sheet of paper; the cut
Crystal that holds that one glass of bistro wine that

You savor after dinner. The soul is more renown,
Since we seem to hear more talk about it,

But the more we talk about it, the less it appears.
It is the cartographer, who is an exile, in the vastness

Of a country without a name. The soul enjoys
Sleeping in; although if you reach for it in the middle

Of the night, you'll discover that it has risen early
To take a walk, or to go fishing, or to just pace,

With its boots thudding on the porch, in deciding
Upon which one to do, or both, or neither.

The spirit wants to have finally made a selection
Of which diamond sparkling in the case is the one

To choose. But the soul, when it is time to turn
Around, and to access the presence in order to look

Into the perpetuity in your lover's eyes, is the Puccini
In our lives. It is the *Nessun Dorma* playing without

A tenor and an orchestra. Although it is the music
Of the vision, it is also the vision of the music.

Shades of Green

It is elegantly furled
        as if it were a broad leaf curled
                into a bright green body with

a tail. Its head is cocked and its
        antennae are splayed, perhaps,
                not so much in consternation

as in consideration of what
        to do next. Its four lime green
                legs attach themselves to storm

window glass, as if it is in
        perpetual mid-leap, inside-
                looking-out of the half-lifted

storm window, that accommodates
        the air conditioner. When I first
                saw it, I thought it was on

the outside of the glass, which it
        may have been, but now it is
                on the inside of the glass, and

if a grasshopper could be said
        to be keening, then that is what
                it is doing. I look out at it from

where it rests on the clear pane,
        the deep green leaves of a maple
                in full view, and beyond that

the sunnier green
        of the open field before
                the windbreak's hedgerow green.

The Victrola on the Label

Mrs. Kevetchan and my grandmother would bask
Together, each in her own chaise lounge,

In the afternoons in Miami in the 1950s,
And sip iced drinks through a straw from

Pastel-colored aluminum or plastic containers.
They would do so sometimes after a morning

In the kitchen making dozens of perogies,
Consisting of potato or prune fillings, that would

Be followed by their having lunch, which
Would often include boiled chicken

Or *gwumpki,* cabbage leaves rolled with ground
Beef. There beneath the mango tree

They would revel in the intoxicating Floridian
Sunshine, each in their housecoats with faded

Tulips and daffodils, that alerted me
To their sadness regarding their deceased husbands.

They would languish together reminiscing about
How lucky they were to leave Eastern Europe

Before Hitler's tanks motored over the Polish cavalry;
Before Warsaw was cordoned off and made into

A ghetto of death; before the black smoke rose
Into the wound that was cut into the sky

From the smokestacks in the camps of barbed wire.
They would recall the days working at RCA,

In New Jersey, where they reminded me
That is where the records were manufactured,

With the image of a little dog cocking her head
Towards the Victrola on the label, as if

To hear the music better. As a child, I imagined
What music the little dog might be listening to,

And it wouldn't be until I was in my late teens
That I would read Chekhov's *Lady with Lapdog;*

Although what lit up my child's mind
With tantalizing delight was Mrs. Kevetchan

Asking me if I wanted to see her *little doggie,*
To which I would display my avid pleasure;

And how she would reach for her purse,
Then open it, and lift up her toy Chihuahua,

Whose miniscule body would tremble and shake
On his miniature legs, his bulging eyes shining.

Only to return him to the large pocketbook
Next to her lounge chair, where she assured me

The dog would be kept safe and cool. Whenever
I recall Mrs. Kevetchan and her little dog,

I think about the wonder of her life, that she
Savored afternoons beneath a mango tree

In a land Ponce de Leon discovered in his search
For *The Fountain of Youth*, for her to have outlived

A job in a factory to afford to retire, and not only
Purchase a pocketbook to outdo all handbags, but

Also to buy a dog small enough to fit inside of it
And to bring it with her wherever she would go.

Glass

I heard a bullet-like thud
  before I had gotten out
    of bed, as if someone knocked

on the glass
  of the porch-side door; but
    it wasn't until later, that I heard

the possibly
  window-breaking thud again.
    A sharp-shinned hawk, that must

have seen the reflection
  of herself, or was attempting to
    pick off one of the sparrows that

nest on the north side
  of the porch. I turned—
    the sharp-shinned had returned to

a leafless branch,
  frisking her feathers and
    rotating her head; fluffing herself,

in her attempt to
  brush away the blow of
    her head-first flight into the glass,

and what might have
  appeared to the hawk as an
    opening through the unobstructed

air. There she was: settling;
  twitching; combing her shoulder
    and wing feathers with the curve

of her beak; and to what appeared
     to be mutual surprise, there we were,
        eyeing each other through the glass.

Bouquet

There are layers of loveliness
to all of this—

this is what the many-petaled
roses know—

imagine that fragrance,
the unfurling

of that which is within their
petals in their opening

to the world; but then again
the fragrance of that is what

this is, which also fills us
with the sweet abundance

in ourselves, as
we open and reopen with

the distillation of that
bouquet further clarifying

each other, as if
we were spiraling upward

toward the light, through
the lattice work of a trellis,

or reaching through
the mirrors reflecting us,

as fluid as water,
for each other's hands.

Augie's

Thank you for the gift of that fancy bottle of the red hots,
with a cork.
They bring me back to my childhood, and to the corner

store in Ansonia, Connecticut, that mill town on the banks
of the Housatonic River, the year after my mother
died. Whereupon, I would visit their front candy counter,

circa 1961.
It was filled with those red hots, real rock candy,
and of baseball cards, with those awful pink squares of gum

that were always stale.
These weren't so much about taste, except
for the rock candy and red hots, but it was the candy aura

that the counter elicited that provided an odd
sense that this may be one of the few places in which you
could at least dream to get away with something.

Nautilus Shell

You have become
old; every winter the cold cuts deeper into your bones.

You have become this
matrix of presence connected to memories—

that biology kit, as Christmas gift,
when you were twelve, that snowless holiday in 1965—

to that lifetime ago
when you were a young man,

the one whose dreams and losses you have eclipsed—
to now, toward the end,

as you hold the hollowness of all that
like an empty nautilus shell, whose spiral mollusk shape

holds everything and nothing, whose resonance within
issues with the sounds of the sea,

in the crashing of waves—
along the coast of a familiar, but otherworldly, shore.

The Gate Left Open

The Black Angus bull
and several cows crunch the snow in the barnyard,

having escaped from the pasture
across the town road—through the gate left open.

The cows prance through fresh snow,
and convene by the compost pile,

near the barn; while
the bull romps up and down the brick esplanade,

on the side of the farmhouse that faces the pasture,
where these Black Angus

have broken free.
The bull in front of my window,

is beautiful and terrifying, at once, its massive dark
shape bouncing from

front to rear hooves; darting through snow;
steam issuing from its nostrils in the sunlit cold

of late morning; loose, unrestrained;
now enabled to realize how large he actually is,

freely bounding—
his pound by pound adding up to what is

probably a ton; seemingly,
feeling at one with the expanse of the open land

beyond what is the partially electrified fence,
which I learn of later, that held them captive.

Now the bull rejoins his harem, and leads them—
since it is rutting season, as I just heard his bellows

and their huffing cries earlier in the day—
out into the south meadow, and they follow him,

strutting on their way—
until two men, who work at Brookfield Farm,

come with shovels to coax
them back from what they might have sensed to be

a trackless acre of fenceless
 paradise, to trot back across the barnyard and over

the icy road, the ground
thundering with the tonnage of their bodies.

Sooey

The time the drove escaped from their pen from the farm
across the road, they moved in a huddle over the lawn,

red-cheeked and pink in their muddied nakedness, cheery
in their sanguine abandon, snorting in their anticipation

of their approaching the compost pile beside the barn.
They jiggled when they moved, ears cocked,

ruddy-faced, in their collective charge forward together,
insouciant in their newfound freedom, just the *oh, yes*

of them a pleasure to observe in their open delight that
was as sheer of a thing as they were of a weighty heft.

Gregarious in their gait together in their small herd, they
launched themselves forward with an intelligence that

seemed to be fertile in their brains, more so, than other
animals, apparently protective of each other as they were

of themselves, seemingly motivated in that they bore
resemblance more to humans, especially in the glib look

on their faces, and that they moved about in the world
not so much at random but that they had intent, a plan

that included one for all and all for one, in their reaching
the kale stems, apple cores, and still-juicy melon rinds

that they so auspiciously found among coffee grounds
in the compost, before their farmer, smiling broadly,

brought them back to the sparseness of their
wooden pens, spattered with a wealth of mud, as tines

of the farmer's pitchfork tickled them from behind,
the lilt of his chanting call of *sooey* the alchemical charm

to bring them home, their snouts turned upwards, mouths
open, congenially returning, squeaking their nasal oinks,

throaty and full, on the run; the beauty in them, seeing
them come; the joy about them, in seeing them go.

Homage to W.S. Merwin

For over forty years I have read your mystic
whisperings, whose images of troughs

of wind through the pines and of birds
returning home from their voyage across

the sea have filled me with oceanic delight,
with the scent of sea salt and redolence

of the windy piney woods where vision
continues long after the images have been

cast, that blows through me as through
the branches of spruce or hemlock, that

rise in me and raise me up, as unnamable
as a flock of birds that I barely see returning

homeward in the distance, but when
they overtake me, swirling above me

on their tireless wings, beating towards
their roost on this island, they create a wind

of their own, that washes over me, as I stand
renewed in the sunlit shadows of the palms.

Starburst

Sweet hours have perished here;
This is a mighty room;
Within its precincts hopes have played—
Now shadows in the tomb.
                    —Emily Dickinson

Gentians blue the shade bordering the back of the house,
a bird's nest is woven into the slats of an awning
of a second story window, but here is your room stripped

bare of wallpaper, its frame speckled with mortar—
one wall painted yellow and three gray cement, red bricks
baring themselves where the molding would be; and what

surprised me, out of the room's two western windows
is the partial view of Amherst center, occluded
by the mansards of the gabled roof of Town Hall,

the shadows of the shape-shifted pines falling across
your brother Austin's front lawn, in full view of the house,
with pink magnolia in bloom—the closed buds

of their petals curled in tight balls this cold morning in May.
This is where you labored and these are the blue-gray
floorboards you walked in choosing your skirmishes

with the world from behind the battle lines of your verse?
There remains the distinct bells of silence ringing,
their cricket calls that modulate above the incessant

motorized drone of automobile traffic below the tall glass
windows above the street, the sunlit window-paned
shadows crossing the lacquered veneer of your bedroom's

oak bureau and pine writing table.
We have the privilege to view the remnant of your world,
but what would you think of ours now,

and its variations on the theme of extinction?
Would you say that we may have been foolish to trade in
the flaming barrels of muskets dispensing the grape

of their murderous shot in exchange for inseminating
the atmosphere with incendiary pathogens that have
resulted in melting both of the poles?

As clearly as you heard and as far as your visions spanned
the horizons of Lake Hitchcock's rolling hills could you
have possibly imagined our own species progressed

in extinguishing ourselves and all other life on the planet,
as you dampened the wick of your oil lamp
after your hours writing beneath the timbered ceiling

of this mighty room, within whose walls a palimpsest
of layers now themselves expose, as do the precincts
you speak of through which your poems play, replay,

resound, and replenish in their perpetuity from you
and your pen to live in us, not for the sake of posterity,
but in the ever expanding starburst of the moment

that may well cast shadows on the tomb,
but also angle the pillared beams of the full dazzle
of the setting sun that fill these west windows

nearly as tirelessly as the earth's rotation around its star,
as we have such chance to observe you
in the firmament through the lines you have bequeathed

to us in your life, whose auspicious element
of what is past and its own blaze of time beyond
whose rigid confines ring with tones of such sweet infinity?

Aunt Joan

You were my mother's only sister,
and you ever so much wanted what you offered me

as gifts would then be returned to you as love;
especially when you visited after our beloved Julia died,

and you drove from Newark to Connecticut. You
sat on the bed, springs sagging, where only a few nights

previously I went to sleep beside mother, while father
was working the graveyard shift at the factory: your hair

bobby-pinned in those tight curls, the pink crocheted half
hat with a veil, only making you appear more rigid;

your white gloves lying on the lap of your dress, fingers
snapping and unsnapping the latch of your purse, pulling

small monogrammed handkerchiefs out to wipe your nose,
to wipe the tears streaming from your reddened eyes.

It was Uncle Steve whom I loved, admired. Steve,
with the dark circles under his eyes, half of his stomach

gone to cancer, patron saint of patience due to his bulwark
and steadfast loyalty to his being your husband—

always the calm voice, always the kindness emanating
in it. Whether I planned to or not, I would take Steve as

my role model, but it was you that I didn't want to become.
The possibility of that opened me like a bag of marbles

ripping; spilling the tigers, crystals, and cat's eyes that
rolled across the floor and ricocheted into the corners.

The cards you sent me, always sent air mail, were addressed
to *Master* because, as you explained to me, I wasn't old

enough yet to be a *Mister*. My thank you notes were
tardy and answered in cramped handwriting, although

it was normally fluid when I wrote anyone else. It wasn't
as if I didn't try to love you in return, it was just that

I feared I would become as needy as you, stumbling over
yourself to exhibit how much you cared for me;

and more significantly how much you hungered for me to
return your need of my affection.

By high school, the distance between us, your
age, and Steve's passing made your cards all but cease,

until even my father thought you may have died yourself,
especially since you had now lived alone.

However, it was the check you sent to me for the purpose
of my purchasing the track shoes,

that I was receptive, that I did write you back
with something other than the normal amount of uninspired

and lackluster emotion; as I practiced sprints in the backyard
wearing my wings of mercury.

Justice prevailed, I later thought, when I missed placing
third in the league meet by a half inch, believing somehow

if I had been more like Steve, and had been kinder to you,
I could have cleared that bar that wiggled up and down,

before shivering and falling to the cinders beside me.
Aunt Joan, after a lifetime of disappointments, I find you

again surfacing in my memory, and even now I sting with
guilt in my lack of attention to you in my so infrequent

recollections; but I realize that it is you with whom I have been
attempting to make amends all these years, specifically

in my choosing to love a woman who is so similar to you,
and who, like me, was unable to return my love for her.

I would be exhibiting hubris to entertain that I have met
the requisite atonement for my not reciprocating

all of what I refused that you tried to give me, since I will
never know if I have realized what my karma demands.

Ode to Jimmy Durante

Ebullient and intrepid,
you always wore a smile for us even when some of us

had no reason to grin; and
you tickled us with your own chagrin of a nose to take

notice of, after which you were nicknamed, *Schnozzola.*
So, the boy with big ears and the girl with freckles

could look into the mirror again and smile.
Who else would spend a career opening an act with

a song as silly as "Inka Dinka Do"?—
only someone like you, who also supported FDR's

New Deal Program with the song, "Give a Guy a Job,"
that you wrote the score to, accompanying

its playing in movie theaters in the early 30s.
You told the band to *Stop da music,* making it a catch

phrase, when Carmen Miranda collapsed on stage—
even softening that heartbreak with humor,

when she said, *I'm all out of breath,* and you replied
with, *Dat's OK honey, I'll take your lines.*

Comic whose hackneyed language caught our hearts
on the pearl of your tie pin, you

reminded us that *Everybody wants to get into the act.*
Only if you could see how true that is today,

although you encouraged us that if you could
Have a million of them, then possibly so could we—

as you also fashioned Bugs Bunny with that line in
Stage Door Cartoon.

You made us believe in ourselves by just you being
you—always the consummate vaudevillian;

top hat waving in one hand, cane in the other;
at home in the stage lights, eyes trained at the camera.

Since you didn't really have a voice, you still sung us
a song, because you sang so beautifully

we decided to sing along.
How apt, how much in keeping with who you were,

that you closed each performance you gave
by honoring your wife, Jeanne, who died, of all things,

unknown to us, of a heart attack on Valentine's Day.
Only you could instill the mystery at the close

of our show time with you by your saying,
Good Night, Mrs. Calabash, taken from the name

of a favorite town of hers; but then you inimitably
continued, your voice rising in a lilt, making us tear

up, to swallow hard, without even quite knowing
why, when your salutation concluded with

the phrase, *wherever you are,* that always had me
envisioning the night sky full of stars, shining over

the rooftops, where I was convinced that your voice
echoed with such certainty, and which, in that

imagined stillness, you made it possible for us to
entertain that we might just be safely tucked into bed.

Quintessence

Dawn quiet, late August,
on Market Hill Road, as I am finishing

moving into the Robert Francis cottage
that I will forever refer to as a cabin;

and I see them: spotted doe and fawn
walking the road's sandy edge;

and they are so nonchalant about
my sighting them and their seeing me

that I could be one of them.
But it was the fawn's antics that made my

seeing them memorable, with her springing
into the air beside the doe;

the doe observing with approval, the fawn
stepping a few feet, then rising

straight up in the air, front legs tucked,
the back legs fully extended—

becoming all of what it was supposed to be,
and emblematic of itself—

absolute and iconic in that pose;
and indelibly etched in a moment of time,

its energizing spirit cresting through
late summer mist, the chill in the air

emanating more from the naked bounce
of its enthusiasm, portending for me

the grace of the years of living in those
woods; herald who presaged such things

by its vaulting in mid-air with such sheer
delight that it endures as not only an image

within me but also abides as a constant
in the instant of what it inspires—

of what it is to be alive, of embodying
the quintessence of leaping and bounding.

A Glove

My father would embarrass me,
as a teenager, when he would choose to

open the door that said *Exit*, or attempt
to leave through the door that read *Enter*.

My father, always true to his Eastern
European heritage by speaking in broken

English, the adroit master of malapropism,
whose *penny in the neck* sounded

as painful as it was incorrect, although its
image remains impossibly poetic,

and just may have lodged in my psyche to
provide inspiration enough to become

inured to the rigors and arduous circuitries
in continuing in the practice of writing

poetry that offers a harsher currency than
any *penny in the neck* could ever possibly be.

When I find myself becoming lost driving
the maze of highways from Hull back to

South Amherst, where I live amid pastures
and open farmland, and need to stop to ask

passersby on the street how to get to
the Massachusetts Turnpike, while holding

out my highlighted and annotated MapQuest
directions, I find myself positioned

in an inescapable karmic truth in a singularly
inexorable and biblical way:

I am my father's son;
no matter what atonement I have tried

to accrue in my life in relationship to him;
no matter how much I attempt to

squirm out of the hard
fact of my needing to sit in the dentist's chair.

I find myself connected to
my father, as coming from him, as being one—

as one might turn a glove
inside-out, then to pull it back right-side in.

Invocation

My father appears in the dream
wearing the grey ball cap with beige chino jacket,

green work shirt and pants,
and he is driving the Chevy station wagon

through the afterlife.
Its high beams shine their columns of light through

the incessant gloom over the macadam of the bardo,
as my father drives one way, then another:

searching, searching;
but seeking what I am unsure;

and I don't know if he is combing for his lost self that
was abandoned during the years

of the arteriosclerosis and the Alzheimer's;
for the son he couldn't recognize; or his wife whom

he had forgotten had died.
However, there he is behind the wheel

in the afterlife, with the powerful beams of the car's
lights cutting through the thick fog

that roils in limitless smoky curls of the dream,
with the inside light on in the Chevy,

so that I am able to see my father's stoic face looking
out through the windshield in his patrolling

of the vastness of the realm he abides in;
and it is then, *oh,* it is then that I find myself lifting up

a prayer both for him and for every one of us:
that we may eventually come to peace in our unrest.

Ode to End of Summer

Sunlight flickers over the lushness of August,
fills even the slender inflorescence

of stalks of timothy, as a flock
of cedar waxwings flies in and out of the hedge

of honeysuckle. Luxuriant halcyon weather
will give way to the flurry and the early chill

of September busyness not dissimilar to the way
the windy poplar lets go of its leaves in such

a burst and with such flare; and letting go
is what we need to do. What a delight to have

leftover morsels of lobster marinating in butter
from last night's dinner, that I serve over

four toast points, spread with mayonnaise
and paprika; accompanied with a salad

of garden fresh tomatoes, snow peas,
shredded carrot, and sweet onion in olive oil

and balsamic, tossed with julienned basil leaves,
cracked black pepper, and Kosher salt.

I finish the plate with a garnish of two grape
leaves stuffed with spearmint and rice.

To celebrate the relinquishing of summer
only makes room for more appreciation

of what was savored and the harvest to come.
To ready ourselves for the harvest we offer

our gratitude to every bite of shellfish and
the medley of vegetables that

they will nourish us and might place us in
balance with the windy poplar releasing

its flurry of leaves and what may be nature's
harmonic asymmetry, igniting us into verb.

Dinner with Camus

I plate both halves of the omelette, one half for now,
one for later; and hear his voice: debonair, erudite,

sweetly gruff, *Merci beaucoup*, he says; and takes a plate,
then sits opposite me. Switching to English, he asks,

*Why did you put in garlic with the sautéed sweet potatoes
and onions.* I tell him, *It is because I love a woman, and that*

*she loves me, but now we only see each other when I visit her
at her office.* Camus answers that Sartre and de Beauvoir

lived separately. He adds, *It was unconventional; however,
their love perpetuated itself. It lasted; it wasn't a convenience*

that they celebrated, but each other. I ask him, *Did they fight?*
He answers with his eyes, lifts a forkful of omelette into

his mouth, then says, *Since we all argue about life itself, then
why shouldn't lovers argue about love, even if they do so silently.*

Before I can ask another question, he queries me about
why I added the sweet bell peppers and the sun-dried

tomatoes to the omelette, and I reply, *Because I wanted
to sing. I wanted to recollect what was fine about last summer;*

*making dinner for Julieanne. Since I had frozen the peppers,
I wanted to eat them before the fine weather this summer.*

He stares quizzically, but compassionately, then asks,
Why? I push my plate aside, surprised to finish

before him, since I am such a slow eater, then answer,
Because I am passionate about the simple mathematics of the lyric.

He reaches over to help himself to another glass of wine,
and says, *It is exquisite for me just to taste this again*, holding

the bottle of Baron d'Arignac up to the light fading
through the two windows beside the table. *Just like*

Meursault when he makes an omelette after his mother dies,
and has a glass of wine with it, in L'Etranger, I ask, knowing

the scene by heart. *Oui*, he responds, and looks out
into the falling dusk. *Did Meursault fire the extra shots*

into the Algerian, thinking it didn't matter, since he was dead
already? I ask him, nearly feeling a little heady from

a second glass of wine. *It didn't matter at that point, but*
everything matters all the time; what mattered was Meursault's

freedom, unenviable as his decision may have been, he explains.
I want to respond that I follow him, but since I don't,

I say, *Then what about Meursault's sense of freedom*
after he is tried and condemned to death? He eases back

his chair, then replies, *You are a commendable cook,*
and I am appreciative that you know my work so well.

Alerted to his imminent departure, I ask, *Must you leave*
so soon? He responds, *We all must go, unfortunately.*

www.ingramcontent.com/pod-product-compliance
Lightning Source LLC
Chambersburg PA
CBHW022012090426
42741CB00007B/1000